It is our mission to promote children's literacy nationwide.
Through our books, we hope to inspire a lifelong love of
reading by touching the hearts of children and adults alike.

For Remy Rose

A sincere "thank you" to my father-in-law, Wayne Curtiss, who heard my idea while half asleep on the couch one night and has been "all in" ever since. For without his perseverance, effort and sincere passion, these books would not exist.

❖

Special thanks to our wildly talented friend, Don Brown, for his magic with colorization and book design.

❖

IHTBT Publishing would like to thank Scott Fleenor for our logo creation and for lending his creative talents throughout this process.

GREATEST EVER

THE STORY OF A COACH, A QUARTERBACK
AND A COMEBACK

WRITTEN BY JEFF ATTINELLA · ILLUSTRATED BY DAVID BOYD

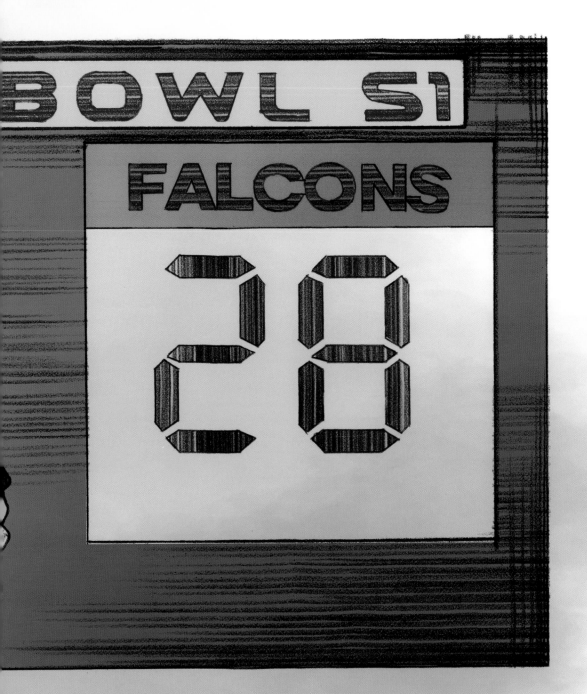

I want to tell you a story,
one that I still can't believe.
The story of a coach, a quarterback
and the greatest comeback ever seen!

...but before we begin, I want to go back in time,
back to the 2000 NFL Draft and pick 199.

The New England Patriots were on the clock,
day two, round six.
Bill Belichick drafted quarterback Tom Brady
with one of his last picks.

YEAR COACH

Coach Belichick was new, his first year as coach,
he ushered in a new era with a no nonsense approach.

Brady was a player from Michigan, whom no one gave a chance.
Other teams passed him up, believing he wasn't worth a glance.

...but it didn't take long for these two men to impress,
Belichick and Brady together were an instant success!

New England won Super Bowl 36 in the pair's second year,
a coach and quarterback combo other teams grew to fear!

A dynamic duo, they transformed that Patriots team,
from a franchise never winning, world champions now their theme.

In a nail-biter of a game,
they caged the Panthers in Super Bowl 38.
When they beat the Eagles in Super Bowl 39,
everyone knew they were great.

Many thought their time had passed
but they held their own just fine.
They beat the Seahawks ten seasons later,
to win Super Bowl 49.

Earning four championship rings
made this duo elite,
but it was Super Bowl 51 that
would be their greatest feat.

That brings us to the crazy season of the year 2016,
which started as a nightmare, but ended as an incredible dream.

Commissioner Roger Goodell suspended Tom until the fifth game,
all because of some deflated footballs. Oh Roger, that was lame!

...but after a three and one start, there was no reason to worry,
Coach Belichick had the team back to first place in a hurry.

When Brady returned, there was no stopping this team.
"We want number five!" all the fans would scream.

The Patriots made the playoffs with relative ease,
then won the AFC Championship;
whooping Pittsburgh was a breeze!
Off to Houston, where Super Bowl 51 would wait,
against the Atlanta Falcons whose offense was great.

Looking to make history, Belichick and Brady were ready to thrive.
No quarterback-coach duo had ever won number five.

The ball kicked off and the game was underway,
if Brady led the Pats to victory, he'd be the best to ever play!

The first quarter drew to a close; the game started off as a bore.
Both teams punting back and forth, zero-zero was the score.

That wouldn't last long because the Falcons got hot.
They started the second quarter on fire, while the Patriots did not.

Before you could blink, the Patriots were down 21!
Atlanta had three touchdowns, New England had none.

The Patriots managed a field goal, as the first half came to a close.
Tom Brady seemed frustrated, he kept missing on his throws.

The second half got underway, but it was more of the same.

Atlanta scored another touchdown, it became a blowout of a game!

Midway through the third quarter, the score was 28-3. The mighty Patriots down by 25, how could this be?

Brady responded and led the team to a touchdown,
but a missed extra point caused Coach Belichick to frown.

He called for an onside kick,
trying for a trick play.
It didn't work as planned, things
still weren't going their way.

The score was 28-9, with only one quarter left to play,
a Patriots win here would take a miracle that day.

...but as many times before,
Tom Brady was up to the task.
Like a real life super hero,
"Mr. Fourth Quarter"
put on his mask.

Slowly but surely, he got the team back in the game.
Hitting many different receivers, it didn't matter their name.

Play after play the momentum started to swing.
New England down but never out, they heard no fat lady sing!

The Patriots down by eight, Brady ready to lead,
a touchdown and two points now would complete
the greatest Super Bowl comeback ever seen!

He marched them down the field with the help of a wicked play,
Julian Edelman's catch was the greatest ever, many fans would say.

The Patriots closed the gap with a great touchdown run,
then tied it up with a two-point conversion - man, this was fun!

The game went into overtime
and New England received the ball.
When Brady took the field,
the Falcons feared they had no chance at all!

It didn't take him long to drive down the field for the win,
Atlanta was left crying, agonizing over what might have been.

Quarterback and coach hugged at midfield,
the miraculous comeback complete.

Five Super Bowl wins - the most ever,
making both men elite.

Goodell handed Brady the Lombardi
and Game MVP, too.

...and to think it all started years ago, pick 199, round six of day two.